PASSIVE INCOME FROM INVESTMENTS

Passive Income From Investments

Four Smart Passive Income Streams: Kindle Publishing, Affiliated Marketing, Real Estate and How Do You Make Money on YouTube

Lee Strong

Table of Contents

Introduction

Have you ever wanted to figure out how you can make some extra money without having to take on a second job? Well, look no further because you have picked up the right book! This book will take you through several different passive income ideas that will help you find the perfect idea for you!

Throughout the course of this book, you will figure out what passive income is, the different passive income streams, the secrets to passive income, and several other ways that you can make money from passive income.

There are a dozen of other books about passive income on the market, so thank you for picking up this one. My hope is that it will be able to help you to find the perfect passive income stream for you!

Chapter 1: What is Passive Income?

Before you can get invested in passive income, you have to understand what passive income is. Passive income is going to be any profit you make from things such as a rental property or other enterprises that you are not actively involved. Just like with active income, passive income is typically going to be taxable. However, it will be treated differently by the IRS. Even portfolio income is going to be considered passive income by some analysts, as is dividends and interest.

Understanding Passive Income

With passive income, there are at least three categories that your income will fall under portfolio income, passive income, and active income. Passive income has become a loosely used term as of late, but, passive income is used when defining money that is earned on a regular basis but you do not put much effort into receiving it.

Some of the most popular types of passive income will include peer to peer lending, real estate, and dividend stocks. The proponents of earning passive income will usually be boosters from businesses where you can work at home or you can be your own boss.

Most people associate passive income with gains on stocks, lottery winnings, retirement pay, interest, capital gains, or online work. Even though each of these activities is going to fit into the definition of passive income, they are not going to fit into the technical definition that the IRS has laid out for passive income.

Passive income, even when it is used as a technical term, is going to be defined as net rental income or income that is earned from a business where the taxpayer does not have to participate materially and can even include self-charged interest in a few cases. The technical definition even goes on to say that passive income "does not include salaries, investment income, or portfolios."

Chapter 2: Different Passive Income Streams

You've seen what passive income is, now how are you going to be able to make money with passive income? There are multiple ways that you are going to be able to make money with passive income, all you have to do is find the one that is best for you! In this chapter, you will see multiple passive income streams available to you!

1. Sell an eBook: you do not have to write the next great American novel. You can write an eBook book that is at least 60 pages and you will then be able to sell it and make around $500 a month thanks to online networking.

2. Create a blog and use affiliated links: affiliate fees are going to make it easier for you to earn more money than when you sell an eBook. All you will need to do is focus on putting out content on your website and getting more traffic through social media and Google. Most people are able to enjoy their first affiliated sale within a month of starting their blog.

3. Sell products online: it may take you a while for this to become a good source of passive income, but it is possible. Selling physical products online is going to be very complicated and time-consuming. In fact, it seems as non-passive as you can get. However, thanks to Amazon, it is going to be easier than you think!

4. Invest: investing is one of the easiest ways to make passive income. The only problem with investments is that they don't always work out. If you do not have much experience or access to capital as well as the time that you need to find the proper

investment, you can end up losing money. However, if you can find the right investment, you can make quite a bit of money.

5. Sell online courses with a membership: this means that you are going to have a website that is only for members and is multimedia driven. In the beginning, this is going to be a lot of work, however, it can pay off in the long run.

6. Start a comparison site: you will create a website that is going to share useful content but is also going to review products in the niche that you find is the best fit for you. It is not a bad idea for you to create a comparison table where each product is listed and has a rating on how many features the product comes with. This will provide the customer with all of the information that they are looking for in one place so that they do not have to go through multiple websites just to find the information that is listed on your website.

7. Create a static guide website that has direct sell advertising: when you do this you are going to be creating an all in one guide website that is nestled into a specific niche such as travel blogs for specific travel websites. From there you will go out and find companies that will want to purchase advertising space on your site once you get enough highly qualified readers.

8. Build an app: build an app on iPhone or Android for things such as DIY or even gardening. Depending on what your application does or what you have to offer on it will depend on what you are able to charge for it. Building an app can be expensive in the beginning, but if you are providing your customers with quality content, you will earn all of your money back.

9. Resell digital products and services: you can do this by web hosting or by creating a mobile website. Once you set up a website, you will attract customers and from there, all of those customers are going to be converted by the product's company which means you will take on the middleman position.

10. Create a book review website: this is going to affiliate you to a website, but Amazon will pay you to leave reviews for the books that you read. You will not make much money until you reach a high ranking with Google. You can do this by creating an email list where your reviews are sent once they are up.

11. Create a lead capture website for real-world businesses: this idea will help you make thousands of dollars a month if not more. You should keep the website simple and make it a Google-friendly content site that will have a high converting inquiry form for capturing details. It is not a bad idea to throw in a free report or something that will boost conversions. It may even work in your favor to create a directory website. Because the contact details of various leads can help your local businesses bring in extra customers, you will have enough room to negotiate with these businesses which will help you to receive a higher return.

12. Build an online store for a service while outsourcing the work: this one is easy because all you will be doing is creating an SEO optimized website that people can use to convert their old VHS tapes to USB or DVDs. From there you will need to get it to number one in Google searches. The website should be user-friendly so that the user does not have any questions and nothing is confusing to them. Also, make it so that they can submit their payment right there or through PayPal. You should ensure that you are pricing this service at a premium so that you can make a good profit once you have paid the person you outsourced the work to.

13. Write for AdSense: this will be different than setting up a blog and adding AdSense. Instead, you will be writing and distributing your content to dozens of high page rank content publishing platforms. Each platform will differ drastically on how much you get from the ad's revenue. However, if you're able to put out decent content in niches where there isn't a lot of information, you will see a payoff.

14. Create a niched stock content library that others can use: create a library of something that you think that others would like access to and live off of the royalties. You can do anything from photos, to melodies, to icons. The biggest drawback on this is that it will be geared for the more creative types, but you will always be able to outsource this work to an amateur that is wanting to make a few bucks. The biggest piece of advice that you can take is that you need to build a library that is tailored to a specific niche. For example, building up a library of stock photos for authors or bloggers who are writing to make money online. By tailoring to a specific audience you will be making your proposition clear and that will make marketing easier, and your SEO will get a lot easier too.

15. Create a software that is a simple online app for SaaS: whether it be a WordPress theme or an online productivity tool, you can make a lot of money with a SaaS application. It is wise that all of the serious programming is done by professionals and that you just sell the software. However, there is a lot of debate on what is going to be better when it comes to making money online. No matter if you choose to be an information dealer vs a software seller, you will have to sit down and look at their pros and cons.

16. Make a fake online store and link it to Amazon: this is different than a fake store because there will not be an online store. Instead it is a content rich site that has a lot of product-focused articles and videos. If you find the right products to feature and add them to your affiliate fees, you can make quite a bit of money.

17. Rent out expensive equipment: some ideas of what you could rent out would be photo booths, treadmills, so on and so forth. This is not going to be completely passive, but it will help you to get some rental income and give you the ability to reap the profits. It is best if you stick to something specific and market it through online directories that are free.

18. Become a digital publisher: this idea is simple, build a website and do online marketing while someone else makes your product. When you do this, you will get half of the profits. In a way, it is going to be like creating your own affiliate program.

19. Buy an online business: this can sound too good to be true, but it isn't. All you have to do is pony up a few thousand dollars and then you will have a profit generating machine that will earn you back your money. There are going to be risks with websites that have not had any Google traffic, if the monetization strategies that you use don't work, or even if the website needs more work than you were planning on. Just like when you buy any business, you won't necessarily get a great business in a short amount of time. However, if you can filter out the millions of business for sale and get a good price on an auction website, then buying your way into the passive income business will be easy!

20. License out your ideas: in the event that you don't want to risk a lot of capital in order to create and sell a product, but you have ideas for products, you can sell your thoughts. License fees for unproven and unknown inventors will be a few percent at best. A lot of ideas are not worth anything but they can be used to add value to the market. The downside to this is that you need to be great at networking and pitching your ideas.

There are a lot of other passive income streams you can use. These were just a few that we wanted to share with you!

Chapter 3: Passive Income Ideas

In the previous chapter, you saw some different streams that you can use in order to earn passive income, but, in this chapter, you are going to see several different ideas that you can use to earn passive income. Each idea is going to require very little effort.

Keep in mind that it is possible to make a great living off of one source of passive income; however, it is more realistic to earn small amounts of money from multiple income streams.

1. Earn cash back for shopping: this idea is going to be a great way for you to save money while shopping online. Money saved is going to be money earned. One of the best ways to do this is to use Ebates where you can get a $10 sign up bonus. On top of that, it will give you cash back for every online purchase. As a member of Ebates, you can earn up to 40% cash back at over 2,000 stores. Ebates also has a referral program where you are able to earn $25 for each referral.

2. Look and see if any stores owe you money: the app Paribus is free and can help you track down any stores that owe you a refund for what you have purchased in their store. While this app isn't going to necessarily give you a passive income, it will create passive savings!

3. Peer to Peer lending: this method will be a financing method that allows businesses and individuals to borrow or provide money through an online service rather than going through a bank. For companies such as LendingClub, there is a 4-9% return which will end up causing you to have a higher average return on your

investment. LendingClub allows you to borrow as little as $25 through multiple loans so that you can spread out your risk. Whenever borrowers repay their loans, you will receive a monthly payment which you are able to reinvest or withdraw.

4. Invest your spare change: by using Acorns, you are going to be able to start investing your spare change without it feeling as if you are giving away money you do not have. Acorns helps you to round up any purchases you make on your debit and credit cards to the nearest dollar while investing the spare change.

5. Lower your bills with a saving bot: you can make money passively by using Trim. Trim will look at your accounts and show you where you are going to be able to save more money. Money can be saved whenever subscriptions are canceled that you are no longer paying for. However, Trim also looks at your bills and tries to find you a better deal on car insurance or internet.

6. Rent: you don't have to rent out an entire house, but you can rent out your spare room by listing it on websites such as Airbnb. The income that you make will vary based on where you are located and what you have to offer. Keep in mind that Airbnb will charge a 3% fee that is going to cover any cost that is associated with processing payments.

7. Browse the internet: you won't get rich surfing the web, but you do have a few options to choose from if you want to earn a little bit of money.

   • Nielsen mobile app: this application will give you up to $50 a year just for you downloading their app onto your mobile device.

   • Survey Savvy Connection: this application will pay you up to $15 a month ($5 per device type) which will total up to $180 a year! The only thing you need to do is remain active in the SavvyConnect community.

8. Open a high yield savings account: by opening a savings account, you will be engaging in the safest and easiest investment option with the lowest interest. The low interest makes it less appealing to most people, but you will be able to increase your passive income by opening up a high yield savings account.

9. Advertise with your car: you do not have to deliver food or have passengers in your car because you can use Wrapify. This application will pay you to advertise a business on your car. The app will track your mileage and your location so the more you drive, the more you are going to be qualified for which means the more money you are going to make! You can make up to $400 a month!

10. Invest with crowdfunded real estate: when you have the money to invest in real estate you will see a return quicker. However, this can be expensive and is also risky for most people. Thankfully, there is a cheaper way for you to invest with real estate and it is to use companies such as Fundrise. You will invest your money in dozens of real estate projects without writing out large checks you cannot cash. You will be able to get started with as little as $500 and you can invest in more than 49 different real estate products thanks to the real estate investment trusts (REIT).

There are new ideas for passive income being created every day because everyone wants a little extra money. You can dip your fingers into whatever you think will bring you some extra money but keep an open mind. You never know what is going to come out next.

Chapter 4: Passive Income Secrets

You already know what passive income is and you have seen different ways that you can make passive income. However, have you ever thought about what secrets there are to how you can make passive income? Make sure that you keep in mind that passive income is not free money; it is going to require you to do a little bit of work to get the money flow started. Think of it as growing a flower. You have to prepare the soil and then water it while the plant does the rest of the work. Your biggest challenge will be to find one that fits your skills, resources, and mindset.

1. Whatever you put into your investment is going to be what will be what you are paid. Your income is not going to be based simply on the time that you spend executing your passive income plan.

2. There is no limit to how much money you will be able to earn. You can put your money into as many passive income streams as you want.

3. When you formulate a plan to enter a passive income stream, you are not going to be spending time; you will be investing it.

4. Unlike your job, your passive income is going to you investing time into a recurring profit instead of trading your time for a set amount of money that you receive from a job.

5. Consider writing a book so that you can receive the residuals for the remainder of your life.

6. Take the time and energy as well as the money that it requires to get into several different passive income streams.

7. Consider investing in real estate. Think about buying a nice property or even a commercial building and leasing it out. It may be wise for you to start with a small investment like we discussed earlier and then work your way up to property investments later.

8. Multi-level Marketing or MLM has been a source of passive income for a long time. MLM does not require a lot of money up front but it is going to require you to take time to sell the product. The biggest problem with MLM is that most people shy away from them thinking that they are scams or because they take up so much time.

9. Money will be made where value is created and exchanged. Value will be defined as the benefit that people are willing to pay in order to receive. In other words, when you make money in any way, the value will have been created and exchanged.

10. Value that is only able to be consumed once will not be considered very valuable. You, your time, knowledge, experience and output are all valuable. However, when things are only able to be consumed once such as a service from a doctor or lawyer, then the value is gone because the product will now belong to the customer.

11. Value will originate from people but does not have to be delivered by them. At some point in time in the chain, the value you have will be created by someone. However, a human does not have to deliver it; technology can deliver the value that was created by a person. Another way to look at it is that your landlord worked in order to buy your apartment and make it nice for you before you decided to move in. However, once this process is done, the landlord does not deliver the value to you each day because you wake up in the apartment every day, no matter what your landlord does during the day.

Chapter 5: Passive Income in a Kindle Publishing Business

You already know what Kindle is and that Kindle offers you the option to publish your own book so that you can retain the profits. The more books that you publish, the more money you are going to receive. Eventually, you will have the option to create a team of outsourced help that will automate your system. While this is a simplified process, it is the same business model that others have used and it has proven to not only work but grow the more you publish.

How Much Money Can You Make?

When you use Kindle publishing, how much you make will depend on what you price your book at. Therefore, if you sell a book for $2.99 then you will receive 70% of the sales which means you will receive $2.09 for every book sold. The only way that you will be able to do this is to have a book that will encourage people to buy it.

Once you've done that, you will need to pick how many books you want to sell in a day. So, if you want to sell five books a day, you will receive $10.45. If you continue to sell five books a day, you will receive $313.50 a month! The more you expand, the more passive income you will be able to generate.

Amazon will record every sale and make a record of everything that is owed to you. This money will be held for 3 months so that the customer can return the book in the event that they are unsatisfied. After 3 months, Amazon will provide you with an accurate paycheck. While 3 months without a paycheck is annoying, it is going to give you an accurate view of what you will receive in the future.

It does not cost you any money to publish on Kindle, however, when you automate your process, you will see costs in outsourcing the different parts of your publication process.

How to Start Selling on Amazon

1. Review advanced courses. Because so many people use Kindle to publish, it is one of the best documented topics. It is recommended that you go through a guided tutorial in order to skip past the painful points of being a first-time publisher.

2. Study the higher selling books. Look at the different descriptions that these books have to offer and also look at their Amazon Best Sellers Rank. The lower the number , the more books it sells a day.

3. Find your niche. You want a niche that is profitable and not too competitive. Don't forget that competition is a good thing so try and keep the competition and profit base balanced.

Market research

Market research will be the most important step that you complete before you can publish a book. When you do market research, your book has a better chance at becoming a bestseller. There are authors that skip this step because they do not understand how to do market research, but, with websites like Amazon, it is easy to see what your readers are looking for.

1. Search by keywords: get on the Amazon website and type in keywords that are related to the genre that you are writing. A few examples are:
   1. Paleo
   2. Shifter romance
   3. Military
   4. Weight loss

2. Look at the bestseller list: when you use this method, you will look at the bestseller list for books that are in categories related to yours. By doing this, you will be able to find all the top books in the genre you want to write. There are some elements you should look at, so you can create a unique brand in that genre.

    1. Book covers

        1. Colors
        2. Font
        3. Contrast between text and images
        4. Images used

    2. Book title

        1. Words used
        2. What is popular right now (romance, historical romance, etc.)

    3. Book description

        1. Does the description make you want to purchase the book right away?

    4. Inside

        1. Read the first few pages and see what elements are used to make the reader pick the book up and not put it down until they are done with it.

    5. Reviews

        1. What elements do the readers talk about most?

        2. What scenes are mentioned the most?

3. What aspects of the characters and the storyline do the readers love? What do they hate?

4. What are some problems mentioned by readers about the book?

6. Calculate sales: when you look at the ranking of a book on Amazon, you can determine how many books are sold and what kind of royalties the author is earning. Open the Amazon book sales calculator to determine the sort of money that the author receives each month.

After you have looked at everything, you will have a better idea of what type of book your customers are looking for. You will also have a better chance at branding and marketing your own book better.

1. **Timing**: The perfect time to start looking for a writer is when you are prepared to put time into giving them the idea you have for your book. You will want to hire a writer if you do not have the time to write your own book . But, you should not hire a writer if you are not prepared to answer questions they may have when it comes to ensuring you are getting the book you are paying for.

2. **Begin looking**: there are websites all over the internet where you can find a writer (look at the services chapter of this book). If you do not want to hire someone off the internet, then you can go to your local colleges and find a writing program that hires out freelancers, so the students can get experience. Do not hire the first writer that you find! Do not be afraid to look around and find the writer that is perfect for you.

3. **Locate the right attributes**: there are a few attributes that you will want to look at before you decide to hire someone.

1. Curiosity: great freelance writers continuously want to learn as much as possible about their client.

2. Deadlines: you will want to find a writer that can meet the deadlines that you put out there. If they cannot meet your deadline, then you will miss the deadline you have set in place for yourself.

3. Technical proficiency: the writer needs to know how to put a sentence together. They should also be creative and engage your audience. If your audience does not want to read what they write, then you will not make any money off your book.

4. **Compensation**: commit to a mutual trial period. You will want to ensure that you are getting the work that you want.

Pay comes in four different formats. You should talk to the writer about how they prefer to be paid to make sure that it will match your payment schedule.

1. By the word: the writer will charge you based on a number of words. For example, $1 per 100 words.

2. By the book: this will be a price that you agree to with the writer and is one of the best ways to pay your writer, especially if you plan on using them for a series.

3. By the hour: the writer will be required to submit a timesheet that shows you how many hours they worked so you can pay them for the time that they worked. You may discover that you are paying the writer for time while you are putting material together for them to work with.

4. Retainer: when you pay a writer to continue to write for you. You should only do this if you plan on using the writer over an extended period.

5. **Red flags**: with times changing, it is hard to look someone in the eye and get an accurate measure of who someone is. Instead, there are other ways to test your potential writer.

   1. Give them a writing assignment. See if the way that they write is what you are looking for. If you decide to publish what they write, then you will make an agreement with them that you will pay them for what they wrote.

   2. Talk to other people that have used the writer before. See what kind of relationship they had and the technical proficiency of the writer.

   3. If the writer has no technical proficiency and the writer has no clients, that can be a red flag. The only reason a writer should not have clients is if they are new.

6. **Acclimate the writer**: nurture the relationship between you and the writer. You cannot hire the writer and push a project on them without telling them what you expect.

How to sell paperbacks

If you want a paperback copy of your novel, one company you can use is CreateSpace (an Amazon company). CreateSpace will walk you through the process like Amazon does so you can publish your book in paperback. Before you can start, you will go to www.createspace.com and create an account. Once you have done that, you will receive a member ID.

1. Select the blue button entitled 'Add New Title.' From here you will be redirected to the project page.

2. On the new project page, you need to fill out your book title, what type of project you are completing and choose a setup method

   1. Guided: CreateSpace will give you a step by step process to

ensure you are not leaving something out.

2. Expert: A single page experience for anyone who knows the process and does not need the steps to be explained to them. This guide is just a refresher in the event that you have not published in a while. Or, in the event that CreateSpace has changed or updated their process.

3. Your title information page will be where you fill out all the information about your book.

Note: when the publication date is left blank, CreateSpace will place the date that it is published on the CreateSpace website. But, if you have used Kindle then you can enter the date you published on Kindle.

1. ISBN: an ISBN number will be required for your book to be published and distributed. CreateSpace will provide you with four options, but there is a free option you can choose from. It is recommended that you look at the choices carefully since you cannot change the ISBN once it is set.

2. Interior: on this page, you will choose how you want your text to appear and what color the pages will be. You will also have the option to change the trim size for your book. The most popular trim size is 6"x9".

3. The next step is to upload your book. A CreateSpace professional can be hired to upload your book if you are willing to pay their prices (CS professionals start at $349). You can also do it yourself.

    1. Upload your book as a .pdf, .doc, .docx, or .rtf file.

    2. Download the word template and format to the sizes that CreateSpace offers.

4. Cover: choose a finish for your cover. Your cover can either be glossy or matte. Submit your cover art. There are three different methods you can use.

1. Build your own cover

2. Professional cover art

3. A PDF of your cover

5. Complete setup: look over your project and make the appropriate changes. Once you are sure your book is how you want it, then you will submit the book for review.

6. Review: your book will be reviewed to make sure it meets the manufacturing and cataloging requirements. You can always order a proof copy, so you can see what your final product looks like, but you will have to pay for the proof copy.

7. Distribution: choose your distribution channel of choice.

8. Prices: set the price for your book. CreateSpace offers a calculator that will allow you to determine what your royalties will be. You should keep in mind that some distributors will discount the price and Amazon will match that price. If you set your price too low you will suffer because of it. On the other hand, you do not want to set your price too high or else you will not make any money!

It is best that you take your time and if you ever get to a place where you cannot figure out what to do, you should contact CreateSpace for help.

How to sell audio books

ACX is another Amazon company that you can use to create your audiobook and publish it. Each audiobook that is produced through ACX will be made available through Audible, Amazon, and iTunes. As the author, you will receive 40% of the royalties.

Here is how ACX works

1. Confirm that you have the rights to the book by looking at the book contract. When you have the audio rights, then you will be the rights holder.

2. Create a profile. Enter a description for your book and what type of editor you are looking for. ACX will ask for a one to a two-page excerpt from your book that will serve as the audition script.

3. Locate a producer. After your post, your producer can audition for your book, or you can listen to sample narrations before you invite the producers that you like to audition for your book.

4. Review the auditions from the producers that are interested in reading your book.

5. Make a deal. You can create an offer for your producer by sending an offer from the "production offer" page. Should the producer accept the offer, then you will have an agreement created on ACX.

6. The producer will record a fifteen-minute checkpoint for your book that you can approve of and offer feedback. After you accept the sample, then the full project will be recorded.

7. You will have the option to ask the producer to make two rounds of corrections on your audiobook. You will now have to choose to pay the producer directly or pay them out of your royalties.

8. ACX will distribute your audiobook. If you give ACX non-exclusive distribution rights, then it will be distributed through additional channels.

9. Promote your audiobook through social media.

10. Each month you will receive a payment from Audible. You can track your progress with your sales dashboard.

Chapter 6: Passive Income in the Affiliate Marketing Business

Before you can get started with affiliate marketing you will need to understand what affiliate marketing is. Affiliate marketing is performance-based marketing where businesses reward their affiliates for every customer that is brought to them through the efforts put in by the affiliate. In other words, you will earn money by promoting a business's products or services and when they buy something because of your work, you will earn money.

With affiliate marketing, there are going to be for people involved in the process.

1. The product creator, who is the company that has a product that needs to be sold.

2. The affiliate network is the hub that lies between the creator and the marketer.

3. The affiliate marketer will be you, which means that you will be the one earning money for every customer you send to the product creator's business.

4. The customer is the last in line and they are the one purchasing the product.

5.

How to Make Money as an Affiliate Marketer

There are many ways to make money as an affiliate marketer.

First, you need to sign up with an affiliate program. There are several different networks that will be there to help you get your start with affiliate marketing. One example would be Amazon Associates. After you have become a member of the program, you will log in and look at the products that are located on the main page of the Amazon site. At the top, you will see a bar that will enable you to grab your affiliate link. Once you grab this link, you will see a drop-down that will show your own personal link that is used to help you make commissions. Another method is to create product reviews. The process is simple; you will find a product that is in your niche and then write a review. The review must also have a call to action button that allows customers to purchase the product through your link. You may place your review on a number of platforms but the most recommended one is through a blog. Another platform you can use is YouTube.

Another affiliate marketing strategy is product vs product. Rather than creating a review, you can create a review of the product's features while comparing them to another product's features. This is one of the best ways to push traffic to your affiliate links because people are always looking to compare products so they can find the best one. This is also going to target buyers that are looking to purchase right now, because when someone looks for product vs product, they want to figure out which one is the best deal. You will be in the position to insert yourself into the equation by providing a more in-depth comparison of the products. The last step is to add your affiliate link.

The last way to make money as an affiliate is to recommend the products that you already use. The best way to do this is to create a 'Recommend' tab on your website. This tab will be where you recommend all of the products that you already use and you can enter your affiliate links beside them so that people can buy them based off of your recommendation.

Chapter 7: Passive Income in Real Estate

Before you jump into real estate feet first, you need to know how to earn passive income from your rental properties and to make sure that you are not spending too much money. Real estate can be extremely lucrative if you do it correctly. It is going to take some effort when you first start out which means that it is not completely passive. But, it will provide you with a monthly income flow that does not require you to take part in daily work.

How Much Should You Spend?

When it comes to buying a rental property, you will want to try and stay stable and in the middle of the road. You shouldn't get too fancy with your first property. Make sure that you can pay cash for the property so you do not have to make payments on it. Plus, it keeps you out of debt. If you are able to purchase something that is priced around 70% of what it is worth, then you will be in decent shape. Remember you are trying to make money on the investment if you can.

Where to Buy?

Most people are looking for houses that are near good schools and in an area with a good reputation. It is wise for you to buy properties that are in solid neighborhoods where the prices have been steadily increasing over the years. You will also be able to attract renters who are responsible and are less likely to damage your property or skip out on paying you.

Rentals that are close to major highways or close to public transportation depots will also attract renters. If you do not want to do residential properties, you can also keep your eyes out for big factories that are moving so that you can rent out offices or rent to a new factory that may want to come into the area.

It is best for you to keep your first rental properties locally so that you are able to keep a close eye on your investment. As you invest more, you can look into rental properties out of state. However, you will only want to do this when you can have someone else manage it.

What to Buy

Before you go out and purchase a rental property, you need to decide if you want an apartment that has regular renters and money coming in for a longer period of time, or if you want a house you can sell for a one time profit.

Buying foreclosures are the perfect way to get a good deal on a property that you want to sell soon after you purchase it. But, you will want to try and avoid money pits or fixer-uppers when it comes to buying rental properly. If you don't plan to manage your own property, then get a property agent that will manage the property for you. You will have to keep in mind that you will need to pay them a commission for the work that they are doing for you.

You should always talk to a real estate agent to see how much rent should be charged to ensure that you are not expecting too much. Rent should come in every month and should be able to cover any expenses such as HOA fees, homeowner's insurance, and maintenance.

Keep in mind that happy tenants will be easier tenants. Always reach out to your tenants to make sure that they do not have any concerns. Try not to contact them too often and do not make any unannounced visits because you should always respect their privacy.

Before anyone moves in, make sure that everything is working as it should and if you are renting out a house, get a professional house inspection before you rent.

When to Invest in Real Estate

Before you start to invest in real estate, you need to be debt free. It is also recommended that you have a fully funded emergency fund which means that you are going to be able to cover no less than 3 months of any expenses. By having an emergency fund, you will be able to fix anything that may come up when it comes to repairs, or if you have tenants that end up not being able to pay one month.

By the time that you are ready to invest, you will be set to deal with anything that you may encounter.

Chapter 8: Passive Income on YouTube

You probably know what YouTube is, chances are you use YouTube almost every day, even if it's just to listen to music. However, did you know that you can use YouTube to make a passive income? With YouTube, you will put in a little bit of work every week (or sooner if that is what you decide) and once you upload your video, you will be making money even when you are sleeping! In this chapter, you will see several different ways you can use YouTube to make a passive income.

YouTube Monetization

You can enable ads which will place an ad before or after your video. You may even place ads in your videos, but most of your money is going to come from the ads that come before the video. There is no selling involved and you do not have to worry about anything except getting views on your video.

In order to enable ads, you will go to the creator's studio, go to the channel, and then go to monetization to enable it. You must have good status with YouTube first, which means you must be partner verified. Make sure all your content is original and try to not post anything that will offend someone.

In order to maximize how much you make, enable the keyword planner which means you need an ad account on Google. Go to this keyword planner, enter the keywords in your video title, and you will see any stats for those keywords. You will also see a suggested bid which is how much people are paying to put an ad in a video for those keywords. Whatever is being bid will be split between you and YouTube.

You'll want to get a lot of views in order to make decent money. Try and stay away from anything that is going to be high in competition unless you have at least 10,000 subscribers or more.

Paid Subscription Channel

Your viewers will pay to view your content or rent videos. This will happen when you have premium content and in fact, it is easier to make premium content on YouTube than on other video sites. This is the content you believe should be shared but should not be free. This would include things like teaching a course on how to complete different tasks, such as how to sew a pair of pants.

To create a paid channel you can go to YouTube "help" to find steps that can help you to create a paid channel. Make sure you have good copyright status and community guideline status. It can also be found on the status and features settings page; this can be enabled here. Make sure you are looking at your tax status before you do this! It may benefit you in the long run.

Affiliate Marketing

This was talked about in the previous chapter. YouTube is a great channel that will drive traffic to your links. This can be recommendation videos, demonstration videos, or anything that will drive people to purchase the product!

Place your link in the first sentence of your video description! This makes it easier for people to find your link and makes it more likely for people to purchase the product you are promoting. Always make sure that people can find the link in the description.

App and rewards program referrals

You will be trying to get people to download and try different apps that will pay you money for every person that downloads and uses the app. You can get paid through PayPal or trade in your points to receive gift cards. You can also use this to watch videos or to take surveys.

If you do this, it is recommended that you do a demonstration on how to use the application and then in your description of your YouTube video, enter your referral number so that others are able to tell the app that you are the one who sent them.

Each application will be different based on the referral points. Some give you 50% of what your referral makes, but other applications will be different.

People are more likely to try the apps that you are recommending, over paying money that will have to be spent with affiliate marketing.

Conclusion

Passive income can be used by anyone and as you saw in this book, there are a dozen or more ways that you can make a passive income. The only thing that is going to stop you from making a passive income will be the work that is required to get it started. Remember that your passive income is going to be based on how much work you place into it.

You should not be scared away from passive income because some of them require you to put down money; there are plenty of other passive income streams that do not require you to put down any money. There are even some that require you to put down what you are able to so that you do not go into debt.

Don't pass up on passive income just because of what some of the streams are. Passive income will help you out more than you think it will! It can even end up helping you quit your job if that is something you are looking to do!

Thank you for downloading this book and if it has helped you, please leave a review on Amazon!